PLANTS AND PLANTEATERS

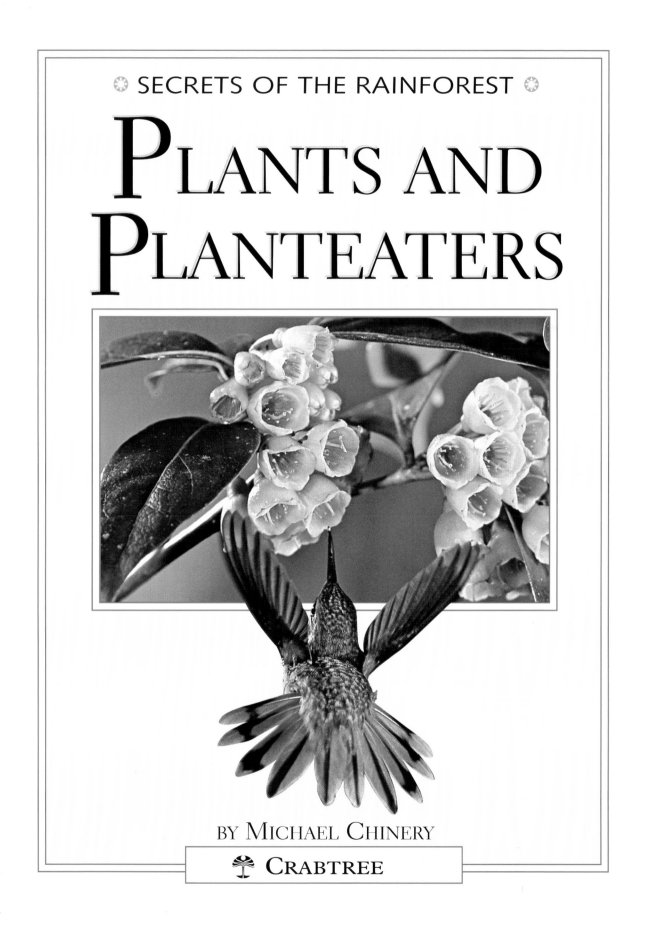

BY MICHAEL CHINERY

🌳 CRABTREE

Crabtree Publishing Company

PMB 16A, 350 Fifth Avenue
Suite 3308
New York, NY
10118

612 Welland Avenue
St. Catharines, Ontario
Canada L2M 5V6

Created by
Cherrytree Press

Library of Congress Cataloging-in-Publication Data

Chinery, Michael.
    Plants and planteaters / by Michael Chinery.
        p. cm.– (Secrets of the rainforest)
Summary: Describes food chains and webs that exist in tropical rainforests around the world.
    ISBN 0-7787-0218-9 (RLB) – ISBN 0-7787-0228-6 (pbk.)
1. Rain forest plants–juvenile literature. 2.Rain forest animals–juvenile literature. 3.Herbivores–Juvenile literature.[1. Rain forest plants and animals – habitats.] I. Title.
    QK938 .R34C44 2000
    578.734–dc21

LC 00-020391
CIP

Co-ordinating Editor: Ellen Rodger

Designed and produced by A S Publishing
Editor: Angela Sheehan
Design: Richard Rowan
Artwork: Malcolm Porter
Consultant: Sue Fogden

Acknowledgements
Photographs: *All by courtesy of Michael & Patricia Fogden with the following exceptions: BBC Natural History Unit 9 top, 22, 22/23 top, 24, 25, 26/27 bottom, 28, 29*

1234567890 Printed in Hong Kong by Wing King Tong Co. Ltd 543210

❂ CONTENTS ❂

PLANTS AND PLANTEATERS   4

FOOD FROM THE FOREST   6

CLIMBERS AND PERCHERS   10

BEAUTIFUL BUTTERFLIES   12

FEATHERED POLLINATORS   16

FEATHERED FRUIT-EATERS   18

HANGING IN THE TREES   20

BROWSERS BIG AND SMALL   22

FOREST ACROBATS   24

GLOSSARY   30

INDEX   32

❂ PLANTS AND PLANTEATERS ❂

TROPICAL RAINFORESTS grow in parts of the world where it is hot and wet (see map page 31). **Tropical** rainforests need average temperatures above 77°F (25°C) every month, and they need at least 80 inches (200 cm) of rain every year. These conditions occur only near the **equator** – in the region called the tropics.

The wettest tropical rainforests get heavy rain almost every day. Some get drenched with over 236 inches (600 cm) in a year. The trees growing in them stay green all through the year. Forests further away from the equator get less rain. For a few weeks, they may not get more than an occasional shower. Some of the trees growing in those forests are **deciduous**.

CARPETS OF TREES

The trees in a tropical rainforest grow so close together that from above, the forest looks like a green carpet. This carpet is about 98 feet (30 meters) above the ground. Some trees are even taller and stand above the others like giant umbrellas.

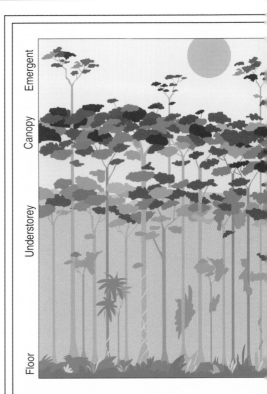

Emergent
Canopy
Understorey
Floor

▲ The layers of a rainforest.

▼ This rainforest in Central America is shrouded with mist for much of the time. It is called a *cloud forest*. Everything is dripping wet, but these conditions are ideal for plant growth.

FOREST LAYERS
• • • • • • • • • • • • • • • • • • • •

THE MOST important layer in the rainforest is the canopy. The canopy is a dense layer of spreading leaves and branches, forming the roof of the forest between 82 and 115 feet (25 to 35 meters) above the ground. It is the factory of the forest, where almost all of its food and energy is produced. Most of the forest's flowers and fruits grow here, and most of the animals live here as well. Here and there, a few trees grow above the canopy, like towers sticking up from the roof. They are called **emergents** and in the Asian forests some of them reach heights of about 230 feet (70 meters). Below the canopy there is usually an **understorey** of smaller trees with narrow crowns. Many of these are young trees trying to reach the canopy. Closer to the ground, there are fungi, ferns, and small flowering plants.

It is quite dark inside the rainforest because the **canopy** of overhead branches shuts out most of the light. It is also very quiet and still, because not much wind penetrates the canopy. Not many plants can grow on the gloomy forest floor, so it is usually easy to walk through the rainforest. Dense 'jungle' develops only along the river banks and where big trees have fallen and allowed light to reach the ground.

AMAZING VARIETY

Tropical rainforests are the richest places on earth for plant and animal life. **Biologists** believe that more than half of the world's plant and animal species live in these forests. The American rainforest is particularly rich in **biodiversity**. Over one third of the world's bird species live there. Two and a half acres (one hectare) of South American rainforest may contain over a hundred different kinds of trees. One reason for the richness of the forests is the fact that they are very old. They have existed for millions of years, unaffected by the ice ages and other climatic changes that have periodically destroyed forests in other parts of the world.

◀ Not all rainforests grow in hot, tropical areas. As long as there is enough rain, they can grow in cooler places. This rainforest, filled with tree ferns, is in southeastern Australia, well outside of the tropics.

◉ FOOD FROM THE FOREST ◉

TREES AND OTHER green plants all make food by a process called **photosynthesis**. The word photosynthesis means 'making by light'. The process takes place only in sunlight. In the rainforest, it nearly all takes place in the sunlit canopy. The green color in the leaves soaks up the sun's energy and uses it to combine water – from all the rain – with a gas called **carbon dioxide** taken from the air.

▼ This fallen tree (below) shows what shallow roots the rainforest trees have, and also how far they spread from the base of the trunk.

FIRM ANCHORS

RAINFOREST soils are usually shallow. Forest trees need to spread their roots over a wide area to stay upright. Many of the larger rainforest trees have massive roots called **buttress roots**. These look like walls growing out from the bases of the trunks (left). They are common on the biggest trees that grow above the canopy and get blown by the wind. The buttresses stop the trees from being blown over.

Stilt roots sprout from near the bases of some tree trunks and grow down into the soil. They act like ropes that hold the trees firmly in the ground. The original base of the tree may rot away, but the upper part lives on, supported entirely by its stilt roots. Stilt roots occur mainly on the smaller trees and especially on those growing in waterlogged soils.

The photosynthesis process produces sugar, which the trees then mix with **minerals** from the soil to make the **nutrients** they need for their growth. Without the rain, the rainforest trees would not grow fast and tall.

▲ Caterpillars like this monarch butterfly larva are eating machines, devouring twice their weight every day.

The food that the trees make provides food for forest animals. Some animals eat the tree leaves or suck the nectar from flowers. Other animals eat the fruit, or the seeds. Because it is warm all year, rather than in a single season, there is a continuous supply of flowers, fruits and seeds. Some insects and birds in the rainforest feed on just one kind of flower. The animals carry **pollen** from flower to flower to help them produce seeds. Sometimes, the relationship between plant and animal is so close that they could not survive without each other.

FOOD CHAINS

The forest plants provide food for the planteating animals. Planteating animals in turn, become food for meateating animals. An ant may eat a plant's seeds and be eaten by a bird which is eaten by a rainforest cat. This is an example of a simple food chain. There are many complicated food chains in a rainforest but they all depend on plants. When an animal dies, its body decays and enriches the soil which is used by the plants, and so the cycle continues.

THE FOREST FLOOR

The floor of the rainforest is dark, damp and very warm, although not as hot as neighboring areas outside the forest. Decay happens quickly under these conditions and dead leaves rarely accumulate on the ground as they do in the temperate forests of North America. Rainforest soils are thin. **Fungi** and **microscopic bacteria** quickly rot the fallen leaves. Giant snails and pencil-sized millipedes with hundreds of legs also eat their way through the dead leaves and fallen fruit. Termites and beetles quickly eat fallen twigs and other timber. The plant-eating animals of the forest floor provide a lot of food for predatory creatures, such as scorpions and centipedes. Many birds also feed on the forest floor. Some eat only fallen fruits and seeds, but most eat insects and other small animals as well.

WATERY FORESTS

Where rainforests sweep down to the sea or to river mouths, big trees give way to shorter ones called **mangroves** that grow in the mud between high and low tide levels. These areas are called mangrove swamps.

HOUSE PLANTS

NOT many plants can grow on the forest floor because the canopy shuts out most of the light that they need to make their food. The plants that do grow there have dark leaves, often tinged with red or purple. These darker colors help the leaves to absorb the light more efficiently. Several of the plants adapted for life on the forest floor, including the African violet (above), make good house plants because they can cope with low light levels indoors.

GIANT FLOWER

THE world's biggest flower is the rafflesia. It may be as much as 3 feet (1 meter) across and weigh up to 15 pounds (7 kg). The plant is a parasite that steals its food from a liana (see page 10). Hair-like threads growing inside the roots and stems of the liana soak up food and then form a flower bud. The bud bursts through the stem of the liana at ground level and opens after several weeks. The flower (left) smells of rotting flesh and this attracts small flies that that do the work of **pollination**. Rafflesia is an **endangered species**, growing only on the islands of Borneo and Sumatra in Southeast Asia.

▼ Curassows live in the forests of tropical Central and South America. They eat fruit and insects. Smaller curassows feed in the trees, but larger ones, including this Salvin's curassow, feed on the ground.

FISH IN THE FOREST

Parts of the Amazon rainforest are flooded for about six months of the year. The rivers carry so much water at this time that they burst their banks. Water up to 32 feet (10 meters) deep floods into the forest and takes the river life with it. The fig tree (left) is growing in one of these flooded areas. Fish take the place of birds, exploring the tree trunks and submerged plants, and feeding on falling fruits and seeds. Insects and spiders have to climb up into the canopy, but many of them fall and these are also eaten by fish.

In mangrove swamps, tangled roots that look like upturned baskets anchor the trees firmly in the mud and prevent the river tides from sweeping them away. **Oxygen** is in short supply in the waterlogged mud, so many mangroves have special breathing roots that stick up from the mud. When the tide is out they look like forests of pencils.

Mangrove swamps are full of animals. Many small animals feed on the leaves or **debris** trapped around the tree roots. Bigger animals, including snakes, feed on smaller animals.

The seeds of some mangrove trees **germinate** before they fall from the branches. A tough, pointed root grows down from the seed and the whole thing looks like a thick dart, up to 20 inches (50 cm) long. When the seed eventually falls, the root is driven far into the mud. Firmly anchored in this way, the seedling starts to grow immediately, with no risk of being washed away by the tide.

☸ CLIMBERS AND PERCHERS ☸

RAINFORESTS ARE full of climbing plants called **lianas**. Almost every tree has at least one liana wrapped around it. A liana begins life as a seed sprouting on the forest floor. Its slender, snake-like stem sprawls over the ground until it finds a tree or a bush that it can climb. Twining around the trunk or sprawling over the branches, the liana grows rapidly upwards toward the canopy. Once it reaches the sunlight, it produces flowers and fruits just like the surrounding trees. Lianas also send out a lot of wiry branches that snake from tree to tree and bind them all together in a dense network. Many of these branches drop down to the ground before finding another tree to climb. Apes and monkeys find these 'bush-ropes' convenient for swinging through the forest.

AIR PLANTS
Not all rainforest plants grow in the soil. Many of them grow on the trunks and branches of trees. These perching plants are called **epiphytes**. They include many beautiful orchids as well as ferns and plants called **bromeliads**, which are relatives of the pineapple.

◀ Lianas hang down from the forest canopy and twine around the tree trunks like thick ropes.

TREE-TOP SWAMPS
• •

THE canopy of a rainforest with bromeliads and stag's-horn ferns is in some ways like a swamp because the plants hold so much water in their crowns of leaves. Hundreds of different kinds of tree frogs (right) breed in these tree-top pools. Most of them spend all their lives in the trees and never come down to the ground. Suction pads on their toes help them cling to the shiny leaves. Many mosquitoes also breed in the tree-top pools and their wriggly larvae provide food for the frogs' tadpoles. Colorful worms called flatworms also live in the tree-top swamps and glide over the wet leaves and branches in search of food.

▼ Clinging tightly to a tree trunk, these clusters of epiphytic ferns hold stores of water at the bases of their leaves.

▼ Small epiphytic palms almost completely conceal the tree trunk on which they are growing.

▶ One of thousands of epiphytic orchids growing in the world's rainforests is perched in the canopy.

The tiny seeds of orchids and spores of ferns are blown by the wind, into bark crevices of rainforest trees. Larger seeds may be dropped by animals. They take root in the dead leaves and other debris trapped on the branches. Epiphytes are called air plants because they seem to live in the air, but they actually grow just like other plants. Getting water is no problem because it is all around the plants. Many orchids have spongy roots that hang freely in the air and soak up the rain that falls on them. Bromeliads and many ferns have cup-like leaf bases that catch the rain. Minerals come from the dead leaves and animal droppings trapped around the bases of the plants. Epiphytes do not take food from the trees and normally do not harm them, but the weight of too many epiphytes may bring the branches crashing down.

Strangler Figs

● ● ● ● ● ● ● ● ● ● ● ● ● ● ● ● ● ● ●

STRANGLING figs of one kind or another grow in all the rainforests. A strangler starts life as an epiphyte. Its seeds **germinate** on the branch of a rainforest tree, but it soon sends long roots snaking down the trunk and into the ground. These roots take water and minerals from the soil like those of any other tree. They branch and thicken, and eventually surround the trunk of the supporting tree like a cage (left). At the same time, the foliage of the fig grows thick and strong and smothers the leaves of the supporting tree. The tree gradually dies and rots away, leaving the strangler growing in its place.

Plants that Eat Insects

● ● ● ● ● ● ● ● ● ● ● ● ● ● ● ● ● ● ●

PITCHER plants have leaves designed to trap insects. The leaf is like a jug or pitcher with a lid at the end. With the lid open, the trap is set. Sugary **nectar** around the pitcher rim attracts flies and other insects. Once they set foot on the inside of the pitcher they are doomed. Unable to get a grip on the waxy surface, they slide down into the pool of digestive juices inside the pitcher. These juices are produced by the walls of the pitcher and they quickly reduce the insects to empty shells. The digested flesh of the insects is soaked up by the walls of the pitcher and used to feed the whole plant.

❀ BEAUTIFUL BUTTERFLIES ❀

THOUSANDS OF different trees and plants grow in the rainforest. Their flowers provide nectar for thousands of different kinds of butterflies. Whatever the time of year, there are always some plants in flower. Most of the flowers are high up in the canopy and most of the butterflies live there as well. They include the world's biggest and most colorful butterflies, some of which glide over the canopy on wings up to 11 inches (28 cm) across.

QUICK CHANGES

The year-round warmth enables the rainforest butterflies to produce several generations, or broods, every year. Some butterfly **species** can grow from egg to adult in just three weeks.

▼ The common birdwing butterfly, of southern Asia, has a wingspan of over 6 inches (15 cm), but some of its relatives are nearly twice as big.

▶ Caterpillars eat millions of leaves in the rainforest. They are the prey of many forest predators, such as birds and reptiles.

Insects living in the cooler parts of the world often need a whole year to complete their life cycles. **Evolution**, which is the process by which plants and animals gradually change from one generation to another, can then take place much more quickly among the tropical insects than among those living in cooler areas. This is one reason why there are so many more insect species in the tropical forests than in the cooler parts of the world.

▶ Owl butterflies get their name from the large eye-like markings on their wings. Up to 8 inches (20 cm) across their outstretched wings, these butterflies fly mainly at dusk and are often mistaken for moths.

FUSSY EATERS

Butterflies are very choosy where they lay their eggs. Each species has a plant where they lay them. The tiny eggs grow into **larvae** called caterpillars. The caterpillars feed on the plants they are born on and will eat no others. The leaf-eating caterpillars are often so numerous that their droppings fall like rain. Some droppings reach the forest floor, but many are caught up in the branches and they help to nourish the perching plants, or epiphytes, growing there.

NECTAR DRINKERS

Butterflies feed on **nectar** and other sweet liquids, including the juices of over-ripe fruits. Some butterflies also like to drink sap oozing from tree trunks. They suck the liquids through a tongue called a **proboscis**, which is just like a very thin drinking straw. When the tongue is not in use, it is rolled up underneath the butterfly's head.

BUTTERFLY JEWELS

SOUTH America's morpho butterflies are famous for their dazzling blue wings. Up to 8 inches (20 cm) across, they include some of the most brilliant of the rainforest butterflies. It is usually just the males that have these brilliant colors. Most of the females are brown. Morphos feed on over-ripe or rotting fruit rather than on nectar.

GLASSWING BUTTERFLIES

A BUTTERFLY'S wings are covered with tiny, overlapping scales, like the tiles on a roof. The scales give the butterfly its beautiful colors. The wings of some South American butterflies have so few scales that you can see right through them. In the forest it is not easy for birds and other predators to see these glasswing butterflies at all.

▶ Swallowtail butterflies get their name from the little tails at the rear of their hindwings. Many species have become rare because their habitats have been destroyed. This green-spotted swallowtail comes from Southeast Asia and tropical parts of Australia.

MUDDY FEASTS

MUDDY patches on river banks or in other more open parts of the rainforest often attract large numbers of butterflies of many different species. Thousands of butterflies crowd together as they try to push their tongues into the mud. This tongue-pushing is called mud-puddling, but the butterflies are not looking for water – there is plenty of that in the rainforest. They are looking for mineral salts, which male butterflies need for their diet. It is sometimes possible to get very close to the mud-puddling butterflies, but if one insect is alarmed and flies up, the others usually follow in a dazzling, multicolored cloud.

Nearly all the mud-puddlers are male butterflies, and because of this it was once thought that the females of many rainforest butterfly species were very rare. In fact, males and females are equally common, but the females usually stay out of sight in the canopy. Unlike the males, they do not need to gather mineral salts for their diet.

✺ FEATHERED POLLINATORS ✺

FLOWERS MUST be pollinated before they can make seeds. Pollen must be transferred from one flower to another of the same kind. Birds, bats and insects all help to pollinate rainforest flowers. Birds are attracted by the bright colors of the flowers. They drink the sugary nectar. While drinking they get dusted with pollen, some of which they carry to the next flower. In the tropics, birds can find flowers at all times of the year, and many of them feed only on nectar. They usually have long slender beaks for reaching the nectar deep inside the flowers.

COLORFUL HUMMINGBIRDS
Hummingbirds have beautiful, shiny feathers that look like jewels. Many different kinds live in the rainforests of Central and South America. They dart from one brightly-colored flower to another. Their slender beaks are often as long as the rest of their body and their tongues are even longer. Hummingbird tongues curl from side to side to form a tube for gathering the nectar. The birds hover in front of the flowers while sucking out the nectar.

HONEY-EATERS, LORIES AND LORIKEETS
• • • • • • • • • • • • • • • • • • • •
HONEY-EATERS live in the rainforests of New Guinea and surrounding areas. Some have long beaks and all have

long tongues for gathering nectar. The tongue soaks up nectar with its brush-like tip and the nectar runs into a deep groove. When the tongue is pulled back into the beak, the nectar is squeezed out and swallowed. Some honey-eaters can poke their tongues out more than fifteen times in a second to soak up the nectar.

Lories and lorikeets are small parrots. They have much shorter tongues than other nectar-feeding birds and visit flowers with shorter petal-tubes. A tuft of hair at the tip of their tongue mops up the nectar and pollen. The birds sometimes eat whole flowers and small fruits. Several different kinds of lories and lorikeets live in the rainforests of New Guinea and neighboring areas. The bird shown in the photo is a rainbow lorikeet.

▲ The white-tipped sicklebill (top right) is a hummingbird that feeds on one flower. Its beak is made to sip nectar from the curved heliconia flowers, but it cannot get nectar from other flowers.

◀ Hovering on tiny wings, this coppery-headed emerald hummingbird dips its beak into a flower.

▶ Wings whirring like propellers keep this green violetear hummingbird in position under the flowers.

Hummingbirds can also fly backwards. The have flexible shoulder joints that allow their wings to whirr round like tiny propellers at up to 100 times a second. This rapid whirring makes the humming sound for which the birds are named.

Hummingbirds drink up to nine times their own weight of nectar each day, and to get this they must visit about 2000 flowers. Most hummingbirds are attracted to bright red or pink flowers.

• FEATHERED FRUIT-EATERS •

MANY RAINFOREST birds **specialize** in eating fruit and rarely eat anything else. This is possible in a rainforest because there are so many different kinds of trees, and fruit is available all through the year. Birds living in cooler parts of the world can eat fruit only in summer and autumn, and have to find other foods in winter and spring. The beaks or bills of the rainforest birds are wonderfully adapted for picking and opening the many different kinds of fruits.

TOP-HEAVY TOUCANS

Toucans look unbalanced because their colorful beaks are so big. The beak is sometimes as long as the rest of the body. Toucan beaks are actually very light because they are hollow. The large beaks allow the birds to reach fruit hanging from the tips of slender branches. When it has picked a fruit, a toucan throws its head back and the fruit rolls down into its throat.

▼ Toucans wave their beaks like flags to signal to each other. This keel-billed toucan (bottom) is from Costa Rica.

▼ The Australian king parrot (below center) uses its strong beak to crush seeds. It also crushes flowers to drink their nectar.

THE DAZZLING QUETZAL

THE quetzal lives in the forests of Central America. The long, shiny feathers streaming from its wings and tail are up to three feet (one meter) long. The male has a bright red belly, but the rest of its feathers are green and the bird is not easy to see in the forest canopy. The quetzal's favorite fruit is the avocado, whose flesh provides it with plenty of energy. Although wild avocados are not as big as the ones in stores, a single fruit still makes quite a mouthful for the pigeon-sized quetzal. The bird flies straight at the avocado with its beak open and relies on its speed and weight to break the fruit from its stalk. The fruit is swallowed whole and the quetzal spits out the hard woody stone later.

LIVING NUTCRACKERS

Parrots live in many parts of the world and in many **habitats**. Macaws are noisy parrots living in the rainforests of South America. Their powerful, hooked beaks can easily open the thick, woody shells of Brazil nuts. The birds also use their beaks like extra feet to cling to the branches while they are climbing.

▲ Macaws often eat poisonous seeds, but come to no harm because they also eat clay from river banks. The clay soaks up the poisons in the birds' stomachs.

◄ The green honeycreeper lives in Central America and feeds on flowers and fruits. It helps the plants by scattering their seeds while feeding.

HANGING IN THE TREES

MANY TREE-TOP mammals move about by hanging or swinging from the branches instead of walking along them. Some of them can wrap their tails around the branches and use them as extra legs. Most of these tree-dwellers feed on fruits and seeds, but sloths and a few others eat leaves.

LIFE UPSIDE DOWN

Sloths are the slowest of all mammals. They rarely move. They mostly hang upside down in the sunshine, holding on to a branch with their big, curved claws. Their long fur usually looks green because tiny plants called algae grow on the hairs. The plants help to camouflage the sloths in the canopy and hide them from harpy eagles and other predators. Sloths sleep for up to 20 hours a day and use up so little energy that they can live on a diet of leaves, which they digest very slowly. Sometimes they take a month to digest a large meal.

TREE-TOP GLIDERS

Some pouched mammals can glide from one tree to another: a fold of skin opens out to form a wing on each side of the body when the animals stretch their legs. The Australian sugar glider can glide for up to 154 feet (50 meters) with its bushy tail acting as a rudder.

▼ A female sloth has one baby at a time and carries it around on her belly for months.

KANGAROOS IN THE TREES

••••••••••••••••••

THERE are no native monkeys or squirrels in New Guinea or Australia. Their role as tree-top feeders is filled by tree kangaroos and various other pouched mammals. Tree kangaroos feed on leaves in the rainforests of New Guinea.

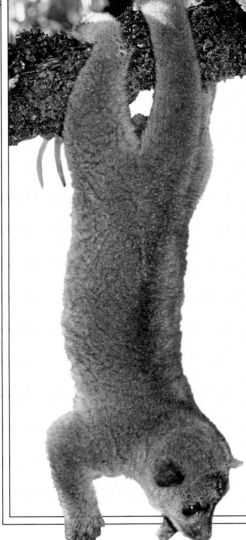

SWEET-TOOTHED KINKAJOUS

KINKAJOUS look like monkeys as they swing through the canopy and hang from the branches by their long tails. They are closely related to bears and racoons. Although they climb well, they do not leap from branch to branch like monkeys. They do not let go of one branch until they have a firm grip on another. Kinkajous live in tropical Central and South America. Most of their relatives are flesh-eaters, but kinkajous prefer fruit. Kinkajous also like honey and get it by poking their 6 inch (15 cm) long tongues into the nests of wild bees. The kinkajou's tongue is about one third as long as its body. Their big eyes help them to see well at night.

They look more like monkeys or squirrels than kangaroos because they do not have the big back legs that other kangaroos have. Tree kangaroos are very strong. They make giant leaps from one tree to another. Like tree kangaroos, the dwarf cuscus (above) is a marsupial. It carries its babies in a pouch at first. It lives mainly in the understorey of the Indonesian rainforest, and eats fruit and insects.

The sugar glider gets its name from its habit of biting into bark and lapping up the sugary sap that flows from the wounds.

FRUIT-EATING BATS

Fruit bats are also called **flying foxes** because many of them have fox-like faces and all of them can fly. Their wings stretch from their shoulders to the tips of their long fingers and back to the tail. They grow up to six and a half feet (two meters) across. The bats sleep upside down in the trees by day, with their wings wrapped tightly around their bodies. They wake up at dusk to feed on ripe fruit and nectar. Fruit bats live in many of the warmer parts of the world, but not in Central or South America. Many thousands of fruit bats gather to sleep in one small area.

THE GLIDING HOATZIN

THE hoatzin of South America is a peculiar bird. It cannot fly well and usually just glides from tree to tree. Baby hoatzins leave their nests at a very early stage and clamber about in the canopy with the aid of two hooked claws on each wing. Hoatzins feed mainly on leaves, especially those of the epiphytic plants growing in the canopy.

❁ BROWSERS BIG AND SMALL ❁

NOT MANY large plant-eating mammals live on the rainforest floor because there are not a lot of plants for them to eat. The browsing mammals that do live there usually live alone or in small groups and they are generally very shy and secretive. They are most likely to be found in the dense vegetation that grows along the river banks and in the forest clearings. Large mammals find plenty of tender leaves near the ground in these areas. Although they feed mainly on leaves, browsing mammals often add fallen fruit to their diet.

SIZE MATTERS

Most of the forest browsers are either deer or antelopes, or pigs. These forest dwellers are generally much smaller than their grassland cousins. Large size can be an advantage in open country, but it is a disadvantage in dense vegetation. The Javan and Sumatran rhinos of Southeast Asia are much smaller than other rhinos. The pygmy hippopotamus is so much smaller than the hippo that it is easily mistaken for a baby hippo.

ANTELOPES AND DEER

THE African bongo (left) is the largest rainforest antelope. It is not much more than 3 feet (1 meter) high, but it weighs up to 881 lbs (400 kg) and, with its horns laid back over its shoulders, it can easily crash through dense vegetation. The royal antelope of the West African rainforests is the smallest of all antelopes. It is only 12 inches (30 cm) high and weighs only 5.5 pounds (2.5 kg). The northern pudu is the world's smallest deer. It lives in the rainforests on the slopes of the Andes Mountains in northern South America. It is about 16 inches (40 cm) high and has tiny spikes for antlers. Deer antlers and antelope horns are usually small in forest-living species, so they do not get tangled in plants.

▼ The okapi's stripes help to hide the animal by breaking up its outline.

STURDY TAPIRS AND AGOUTIS

• •

TAPIRS (above) are related to horses and rhinos. Their sturdy bodies, weighing up to 661 pounds (300 kg), are perfectly built for forcing their way through the dense vegetation of river banks and forest clearings. Tapirs eat leaves and twigs, which they pull down with their short trunks. They also eat grass and water plants.

Agoutis are sturdy South American rodents. They look like long-legged guinea pigs. Agoutis eat leaves and fruit that has fallen from trees. They listen for the thud of fruits falling to the ground and then rush out to find them. People often hunt the animals by throwing stones, which the agoutis think are falling fruits. Their teeth are strong enough and sharp enough to gnaw through the woody shells of Brazil nuts.

The Indian, or Asiatic, elephant is the largest of all rainforest animals. It grows to a height of about 9.8 feet (3 meters) and weighs up to 5.8 tons (5 tonnes), but it is still much smaller than the elephants living on the African **savannas**. Smaller still are the forest elephants living in the rainforests of western and central Africa. These elephants are under 8 feet (2.5 meters) high and are darker and hairier than savanna elephants. The okapi is one of the tallest forest browsers. It is related to the giraffe and grows to a height of nearly 8 feet (2.5 meters). It lives deep in the rainforests of Central Africa and was not discovered until 1901. Even now, few people have ever seen an okapi.

SIGHT AND SOUND

Sounds and scents are more important than sight in the dim forests. It is not easy for animals to see through the trees, so they call to each other instead. Most of the mammals have large ears and a good sense of smell. Asiatic and forest elephants are noisier than bush elephants that live in open country and can see each other coming.

◀ South America's collared peccary is related to pigs. It feeds mainly on roots.

⁕ FOREST ACROBATS ⁕

GIBBONS AND orangutans are apes that live in Southeast Asia. Gibbons live in small family groups in the tree-tops. They are among the fastest and noisiest of the tree-top mammals. They hoot loudly in the morning. Their calls can be heard all over the forest. The hooting lets other gibbons know that the **territory** is occupied and they should stay away.

Gibbons are fruit eaters who get very excited when they find a tree with a lot of fruit. They hoot to make sure that other gibbons stay away from their meal. Gibbons also eat small amounts of leaves and flowers, as well as occasional lizards and other small animals.

OLD MAN OF THE FOREST

The orangutan lives only on the Indonesian islands of Borneo and Sumatra. Orangutan means 'old man of the forest'. Adult males have wrinkled faces and grey beards. Females are smaller and less wrinkled than the males.

▲ A gibbon opens its mouth in a shrill call.

▼ Gibbon babies drink their mothers' milk but soon learn how to pick fruit.

▲ A young male orangutan. Orangutans are endangered by logging and forest fires that destroy their habitat.

SWINGING THROUGH THE TREES

GIBBONS and orangutans have arms that are longer and stronger than their legs. They move through the canopy mainly by swinging from hand to hand along the branches. This kind of movement is called **brachiation** and it requires very powerful shoulder muscles. Long hands and fingers give the animals a firm grip on the branches. Gibbons move so quickly that they seem to fly through the tree-tops, sometimes covering 32 feet (10 meters) or more with each swing and hardly appearing to touch the branches at all. They also walk upright along the branches, using their long arms to balance themselves.

Orangutans (left) are bigger, heavier, and slower than gibbons but they are still acrobatic. They use all four limbs to climb and swing through the branches. An orangutan never leaps from branch to branch like a gibbon. It always hangs on with at least one hand or foot until it can get another good grip, even if this means doing the splits!

Orangutans eat fruit, including hard-shelled nuts that they break open with their strong teeth. They also eat leaves and occasionally catch small animals. Each adult orangutan wanders through a home area, or range, of several square miles (or kilometers). The ranges of other orangutans often overlap, but the animals rarely meet. Orangutans are solitary animals. Each one bellows loudly from time to time, especially in the mornings and this is usually enough to keep them apart.

Occasionally, several orangutans gather to eat fruit on one tree when the fruit ripens. Orangutans know all the good trees in their area. Big males often wander over the rainforest floor, and make their beds under leafy branches broken from the bushes. Other orangutans rarely come down from the trees. Orangutans and other rainforest apes are sometimes caught and sold by **poachers**. Some governments and people are trying to stop the capturing and selling of these animals.

AGILE MONKEYS

Every rainforest in the world is a home for monkeys. Most of them live high in the canopy. Their feet and hands are good at gripping branches, though they tend to run and jump from branch to branch rather than swinging with their arms. Their tails help them to balance. Some South American monkeys have **prehensile tails**, which can be used like extra hands to grasp the branches.

Most monkeys love fruit. They usually eat some insects and other small animals as well and they often eat birds' eggs. Some monkeys, including the curious proboscis monkeys, eat only leaves. Leaves are not easy to digest and the monkeys have to eat large quantities. They need big stomachs to hold all the leaves, and therefore look pot-bellied.

▶ Spider monkeys (right) have long arms and legs to help them move from tree to tree. This monkey is drinking nectar from a flower.

OLD WORLD AND NEW WORLD MONKEYS

MONKEYS belong to the group of mammals called primates. This group also contains the apes and human beings, but monkeys differ from the apes in having tails. Most of them are also smaller than the apes. Monkeys living in Africa and Asia – the Old World – have narrow noses, with their nostrils close together and pointing downwards, as you can see in the crested black macaque (left). New World monkeys, from the Americas, like the silky marmoset (right), have broad noses with well-separated nostrils that face outwards.

► A howler monkey
gives a warning to
other howler
monkeys to
keep out of
its territory.

▼ The South American squirrel
monkey has strong back legs that it
uses to jump from branch to branch.
It eats flowers and fruits.

MONKEYS LARGE AND SMALL

Howler monkeys eat a mixture of fruit and leaves. They are slow-moving animals and spend a lot of time sitting quietly and digesting their leafy meals. Their howling calls can carry as much as 3 miles (5 kilometers) through the forest. A hollow bone in a big throat pouch acts like a megaphone to amplify the sound. Howlers live in groups of up to 30 animals and the howling warns other howler groups and ocelots to stay away.

Howlers are the largest monkeys in Central and South America. Fully grown animals weigh up to 22 pounds (10 kg). Marmosets are tiny. The pygmy marmoset, weighing under 7 oz. (200 g), is the smallest of all monkeys. Marmosets eat fruit and insects, especially juicy caterpillars. They sometimes catch lizards and small snakes. They also use their chisel-shaped front teeth to gouge holes in tree trunks and branches, and then they lap up the sugary sap that oozes from the holes.

The closely related tamarins have smaller front teeth and cannot chew holes in bark, but they often move in to feed when the marmosets have finished. Marmosets and tamarins have sharp claws that help them to climb smooth tree trunks. Other monkeys all have nails on their fingers and toes, like humans.

▼ Like other monkeys, this marmoset has large forward-pointing eyes that allow it to judge distances accurately, an essential skill for animals that spend their lives leaping from branch to branch.

▶ The mandrill is a large ground-living monkey of the African rainforest. The male's colors get even brighter when it is angry.

▶ At rest on a fruit-laden branch, this white-lipped tamarin from Brazil shows the claws that help it to climb.

◀ The proboscis monkey of Borneo uses its big nose to make loud hooting calls. When calling, it lifts its nose like a trumpet to increase the sound.

❋ GLOSSARY ❋

Adaptation Changes in a plant or animal that increase its ability to survive and reproduce in its particular environment.

Air plant A name sometimes given to epiphytic plants that perch on the branches of trees. They were once thought to survive purely on air. See Epiphyte.

Bacteria Very tiny single-celled organisms that exist everywhere in nature and play an important role in the break-down and recycling of dead plants and animals. Many of them, often known as germs, cause disease in living plants and animals.

Biodiversity The variety of species found in any natural region. The rainforests contain more species than any other habitat.

Brachiation The name given to the movement of gibbons and some monkeys that swing through the branches with their arms.

Bromeliads A group of tropical plants, including the pineapple, with a rosette of stiff leaves. Many are epiphytes.

Buttress roots Large roots that spread from the base of a tree like low walls and help to support the trunk.

Canopy The 'roof' of the rainforest, formed by the leafy branches of the trees. It is usually about 98 feet (30 meters) above the ground and cuts off most of the light from the forest floor.

Carbon dioxide A gas in the air that plants use for photosynthesis.

Cloud forest Areas of forest that are so high up that they are almost permanently shrouded in mist.

Debris Fallen leaves and other matter left to decompose.

Deciduous tree Any tree that drops all of its leaves for part of the year.

Emergent Any large tree that grows above the rain forest canopy.

Endangered species Plant or animal species whose numbers have fallen so far that without protection they face extinction.

Epiphyte Any plant that grows on another, especially on the branches of a tree, but takes no food from it. Ferns, orchids, and bromeliads are common epiphytes in the rainforests.

Equator The imaginary line around the center of the earth, midway from the north and south poles.

Evergreen Any tree or shrub that remains green throughout the year.

Evolution The process by which plants and animals slowly change from generation to generation, gradually giving rise to new species that are adapted to different habitats and different ways of life.

Flying fox Any of a number of large fruit-eating bats, with faces very like those of foxes.

Fruit bat Any large bat that feeds mainly on fruit.

Fungi (singular fungus) Organisms, including mushrooms and molds, that absorb their food from living or dead matter.

Germinate To begin to grow. A seed germinates by putting down a root and sending up a shoot.

Habitat The place where certain animals and plants normally live.

Herbivore An animal that feeds on plants.

Larva (plural larvae) A stage in the development of some animals. Caterpillars and tadpoles are larvae.

Liana A climbing plant with long, woody stems that hang from the trees like ropes. Also known as vines, lianas belong to many different plant families.

Mangrove Any of a group of small, evergreen trees with tangled, basket-like roots that grow around tropical coasts.

Minerals Chemical substances, some of which are essential for life.

Nectar The sweet, sugary juice produced by flowers and some other plant organs to attract and feed insects.

Omnivore An animal that eats both plant and animal matter.

Oxygen A gas in the air and in water that is essential to plant and animal life.

Endangered!

RAINFORESTS are home to more plants and animals that any other habitat on earth. They are important to the world but they are in danger of destruction. Many of the animals and plants shown in this book are endangered. Their rainforest habitat is slowly being destroyed by humans. If you are interested in knowing more about rainforests and in helping to conserve them, you may find these addresses and websites useful.

Friends of the Earth
USA - 1025 Vermont Ave NW, 3rd floor, Washington, DC, 20005-6303
Canada - 47 Clarence St. Suite 306, Ottawa, ON, K1N 9K1

Rainforest Foundation, U.S.
270 Lafayette Street, Suite 1107
New York, NY, 10012 USA

Rainforest Alliance
65 Bleecker Street, New York, NY, 10012 USA

Rainforest Action Network
221 Pine Street, Suite 500
San Francisco, CA
94104 USA

Greenpeace
USA- 1436 U Street NW
Washington, DC, 20009, USA
Canada - 250 Dundas Street West, Suite 605
Toronto, ON, M5T 2Z5, Canada

Rainforest Alliance
http://www.rainforest-alliance.org

Friends of the Earth
http://www.foecanada.org
http://www.foe.org/FOE

Environmental Education Network
http://envirolink.org.enviroed/

Greenpeace
http://greenpeace.org

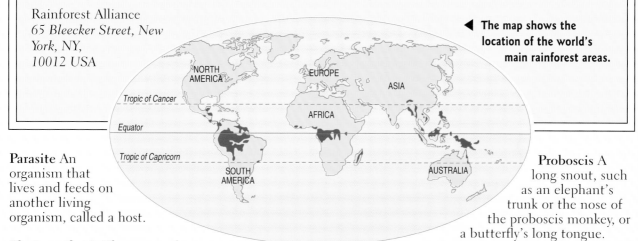

◀ **The map shows the location of the world's main rainforest areas.**

Parasite An organism that lives and feeds on another living organism, called a host.

Photosynthesis The process by which green plants make food. The plants use energy from sunlight to convert water and carbon dioxide gas into sugar.

Pitcher plant Any of several plants whose leaves form liquid-filled traps for insects.

Poacher One who hunts or takes animals illegally

Pollen The dust-like material formed in the stamens of flowers and carried by wind or by animals to other flowers of the same kind. This transfer is called pollination and it leads to the formation of fruits and seeds.

Predator An animal that eats other live animals, as its prey.

Prehensile tails Tails that can grasp, allowing their owners to hang from a branch.

Proboscis A long snout, such as an elephant's trunk or the nose of the proboscis monkey, or a butterfly's long tongue.

Savanna The vast grassy plains of Africa where there are few or no trees.

Specialize To develop, adapt, or concentrate on a specific function.

Stilt roots Slender roots growing out from the lower part of a tree trunk that help to hold it up.

Territory An area inhabited and defended by an animal or group of animals against others of the same species.

Tropical Describes the tropics – the warm areas around the equator.

Trunk The main stem of a tree.

Understorey The layer of vegetation growing below the canopy, consisting mainly of young trees.

❈ INDEX ❈

Page numbers in *italics* refer to illustrations.

A

African violet 8
agoutis 23
air plants 10-11, *10-11*
antelopes 22, *22*
apes 24-5, *24-5*
arms and legs 25, *26-7*
avocado 19

B

bacteria 8
bats, fruit-eating 21
beaks/bills 16-17, *16-17*, 18, *18*, 19
beetles 8
biodiversity 5
birds 5, 7, 9, *9*, 16-19, *16-19*, 21
birdwing butterfly *12-13*
bongo 22
Borneo 24, 28-9
brachiation 25, *25*
Brazil nuts 19, 23
breathing roots 9
bromeliads 10-11, *10-11*
browsing mammals 22-3, *22-3*
butterflies 12-15, *12-15*
buttress roots 6-7, *7*

C

calls, territorial 24, *24*, 25, 27, 28, *28-9*
camouflage 20, *22-3*
canopy *4*, 5, 6, 8, 10, 11, 12, 15, 20-1, 24-9
carbon dioxide 6
caterpillars 7, *12*, 14, 28
centipedes 8
claws 21, 28, 29
climbing plants 10
cloud forest *4*
crocodiles 9
curassows 9
cuscus, dwarf *20-1*

D

decay 7, 8
deciduous trees 4
deer 22
digestion 20, 26, 28
droppings, animal 11, 14

E

ears 23
elephants 23
emergent trees *4*, 5
endangered species 9, 24, 31
epiphytes 10-11, *10-11*, 14, 21
evolution 13

F

feeding adaptations 5, 7, 16-17, *16-17*
ferns, epiphytic *10*, 10-11
fig tree 8, *10*, 11
fish in the forest 9
flatworms 10
flies 9, 11
floods 9
flowers 5, 7, 9, 12, 16, 24
flying foxes 21
flying, hummingbirds 17
food chains 7, 8, 9, 24, 25, 26
food supply 7, 10, 11, 14, 21

forest layers *4*, 5
forest, watery 8-9, *8-9*
frogs 10, *11*

G

gibbons 24-5, *24-5*
glasswing butterflies *14*
gliders 20-1

H

harpy eagles 20
hearing 23
hippopotamus, pygmy 22
hoatzin *21*
home range/territory 24, 25, *27*
honeycreeper, green 19
honey-eaters 16-17
house plants 8
howler monkeys 27, 28
hummingbirds 5, 16-17, *16-17*

I

insects 8, 9, *11*, 26

J

'jungle' 5

K

king parrot 18-19
kinkajous *21*

L

lianas 9, 10, *10*
life cycle, butterflies 12-13, 14
lories 16-17
lorikeets *16*, 16-17

M

macaque, black 26
macaws 19
mammals 20-9, *20-9*
mandrills 28-9
mangroves 8-9, *8-9*
marmosets 26-7, 28, *28*
marsupials 20-1
millipedes 8
minerals, in food chain 6-7, 11, 15
monarch butterfly larva 7
monkeys 26-7, *26-7*, 28-9, *28-9*
morpho butterflies *14*
mosquito larvae 10
movement, apes and monkeys 25, 26
mud-puddling *15*

N

nectar-drinkers 5, 7, 11, 12, 14, 16-17, *16-17*, *18*, 21

O

ocelots 28
okapi 22-3, 23
'old man of the forest' 24, *24-5*
orangutans 24-5, *24-5*
orchids 10, 11, *11*
owl butterfly *13*
oxygen 9

P

palms, epiphytic *10*
peccary, collared 22-3
photosynthesis 6
pitcher plants *11*
plants 4, *4-5*, 5
    butterflies and 14
    climbing/perching 10-11, *10-11*
    endangered species 9
    forest floor 8
    insect-eating *11*
    making food 6

parasitic 9
pollen/pollination 7, 9, 16
pools, tree-top *10-11*
pouched mammals 20-1, *20-1*
prehensile tails 26
primates 26-7, *26-7*
proboscis 14
proboscis monkeys 26, 28-9
pudu 22

Q

quetzal *18*, 19

R

rafflesia 9
rainfall 4, *6-7*
rainforests:
    age of 5
    locations *4-5*
    map *31*
    wettest 4
rhinoceros 22
roots/root systems 6-7, *7*, 10-11
    epiphytes 11
    mangroves 8-9, *9*
rotting/decay 7, 8
royal antelope 22

S

sap, as food 14
scorpions 8
seeds 7, 8, 9, 10-11, 19
sicklebill, white-tipped 17
sloths 20, *20*
snails, giant 8
snakes 9
soils 7, 8
spider monkeys 26-7
spiders 9
squirrel monkey 27
stag's-horn ferns 10
stilt roots 7
strangler figs *10-11*
sugar glider 20-1
swallowtail butterflies *14-15*
swamps, tree-top *10-11*

T

tamarins 28, 29
tapirs 23
teeth, monkeys 28
temperatures, average 4
termites 8
tongues, nectar-eaters 14, 16-17
toucans 18, *18*
tree ferns 5
tree frogs 10, *11*
tree kangaroos 20-1
tree species 5, 20-1, *20-1*
    forest layers 4, *4-5*
    making food 6-7
    strangled *10-11*
tropics *4*

U

understorey *4-5*

W

wings *14*, 17, 21